Roy had a budgie.
He called it Joey.

Joey flew outside.

'Oh no!' said Roy.

Roy couldn't get Joey.

Joey flew away.

Roy went to the wood.

He looked for Joey.

Roy couldn't see Joey.

An ostrich was in the wood.

Roy looked at the ostrich.

The ostrich looked at Roy.

They saw the zoo-keeper.
The zoo-keeper had a budgie.

'It's my ostrich,' said the zoo-keeper.

'It's my budgie,' said Roy.

'Thanks,' they said.